ADDIO,
MADRETTA AND OTHER PLAYS

ADDIO, MADRETTA

AND

OTHER PLAYS

BY

STARK YOUNG

One-Act Play Reprint Series

———

Core Collection Books, inc.

GREAT NECK, NEW YORK

First Published 1912
Reprinted 1976

International Standard Book Number
0-8486-2011-9

Library of Congress Catalog Number
76-40396

PRINTED IN THE UNITED STATES OF AMERICA

CONTENTS

ADDIO

To

Laura Burleson

ADDIO

MONKEY TOM.
HARRY BOYD.
FRITZ.
SUSA.

SCENE.—*An eating-room in* FRITZ' *bakery and restaurant, New Orleans. A few tables; show-cases with bread and cakes; a faded palm or so, and ribands of colored paper; compose the furnishings of the place. Two screens stretch across the back; a door on the left opens into the street.*

[FRITZ *is seen putting the loaves into one of the cases and humming to himself a broken air. He is a German, big, easy-going, blond, with a slight accent.*]

[HARRY *enters, fanning himself with his hat.*]

FRITZ. Hello, Harry! How's your character? Ya, ya, ain't it hot!

HARRY. Fritz, how goes it? I thought I was going to be late. [*He sits down by a table to the right.*] I promised to meet Susa here at six.

FRITZ. It's that now.

HARRY. Just six?

11

FRITZ. Ya, you're all right. How is Susa? I haven't seen her in weeks.

HARRY. Straight and quick as ever, and full of spirit.

FRITZ. Susa's all right!

HARRY. Yes, Susa 'll come out all right, though——

FRITZ. Is she still at the Market yet?

HARRY. Yes, at her mother's stand, the second on the left as you go in. But I'm afraid business is slow for them.

FRITZ. Ach, a pretty girl like dat oughtn't to have no business but a husband. And how is your business?

HARRY. Booming, Fritz! I'm making fifty dollars a week with my teams now, clear.

FRITZ. Fifty dollars! Ach himmel! Why— den you can marry!

HARRY. If Susa will only say the word, I'm ready for it! She seems to love me sometimes, Fritz, and sometimes she doesn't.

FRITZ. Ach, dat's all right. Dey's all dat way. Sometimes dey do and dey don't and some- times dey don't and dey do.

HARRY. She had a sweetheart in Sicily once, and I think she remembers him sometimes; but then——

FRITZ. Ach, nein, she's forgotten him.

HARRY. You never can tell about these things, it may be——

[TOMASSO's *hand organ is heard outside playing the "Merry Widow Waltz."*]

FRITZ. Pst! Listen, dere's Monkey Tom——

HARRY. Who?

FRITZ. Monkey Tom, here he iss!

[TOMASSO *enters from the street, carrying by a strap his organ, which is supported from beneath by a pole.*]

TOMASSO. Buon giorno, signore—howdy!

FRITZ. Well—hello Tom! Don't he speak der English now? Mr. Boyd, Signor Tomasso.

HARRY. Howdy, how are you?

[TOMASSO *bows.*]

FRITZ. How iss dis for weather, Tom? Nearly as hot as Sicily, eh?

TOMASSO. Sicilia, that is not hot!

FRITZ. Ach, Herr Gott, dat is phere dey haf dose cool liddle volcanoes, yes. Didn' you tell me, Tom, dat Sicily vas hot und ugly?

TOMASSO. Hot and ugly—oh cielo, oh, signore! Na, na, signore, I see, signore, you make of me fun.

FRITZ. All right, Tom. You want your bread and the cake for Gigia, eh?

HARRY. Does he buy cake for the monkey?

TOMASSO. How Gigia did love de cake!

FRITZ. Why, phere iss Gigia? Harry, you saw Gigia dance, yes?

HARRY. [*Shaking his head.*] No, never did.

TOMASSO. No, no cake today, signore. Gigia, Gigia's dead—dieda last night—poor Gigia—all I had!

FRITZ. Ach, nein, nein, cheer up yourself, you will pick up less money but you will need less to buy. What is der brod, long or short? To-day's or yesterday's? Today's is 5 cents, yesterday's 2 cents.

TOMASSO. Short, *it* is too mucha wivout Gigia.

FRITZ. Yesterday's?

TOMASSO. Si, si, me no lika today's bread. It is too—too—hot.

FRITZ. Ya, ya, I see—[*Laughing.*]—I see Tommie. Today's brod iss too hot, yes.

HARRY. How do you like America, Tom?

TOMASSO. Me? Oh, I no like America. Fast, so fasta! I say "Permesso, signore,"—he say "Git out de way!"—[*He comes down to the front.*]—and Dio!—domenico, Sunday, no festa, no wine, no——

HARRY. How long have you been over?

TOMASSO. Two year and half. Longa, signore!

HARRY. You've played the organ all the time, eh? Made any money?

TOMASSO. Si, si, but only a little, poco, poco, signore. You see, signore, I am lame and weaka——

FRITZ. Ach, himmel, Tom is getting rich! [*He finds his wire brush and stands guard over the case of bread.*]

TOMASSO. Na, na!

HARRY. Why do you stay then, if you make no money?

TOMASSO. Ah, signore, I didna come for money.

FRITZ. Ach, lieber, what den? [*Striking at a fly.*] for lof?

TOMASSO. [*Excitedly.*] Listen, signore—me —I—am lookinga for someone.

HARRY. A vendetta, eh? to kill?

TOMASSO. No, signore, not kill—to love.

HARRY. A woman?

TOMASSO. Si, justo.

FRITZ. Ach! [*He hits hard and gets his fly.*] dese vomen!

HARRY. And have you found her?

Tomasso. Found her—no, signore, mai, never found.

Susa. [*Outside.*] Eh, Pietro, ecco! Domani arancie e cirassi——

[*At the sound of her voice* Tomasso *starts violently, and, as she enters, retreats to the rear of the shop.*]

A Man's Voice. [*From the street.*] Si, si, ho capito, domani mattina a buon ora.

Susa. [*In the door.*] Si, senza mancanza, va bene.

[*She enters hastily and angrily.*]

Harry. [*Going towards her.*] Susa! Why I thought you had forgotten!

Susa. [*Motioning him back from her.*] Forgotten—io—I? You have forgotten—you say you come for me by the Market—and I—[*Half sobbing.*] I wait, wait till every one goes away—waita, wait, wait, and was afraid to stay longer —and so—so I came—epoi, senta, listen—!

Harry. No, no, Susa, I'm sorry. You got it wrong. I said I'd meet you here at Fritz's. [*She turns her back on him.*] Why, you're not mad, are you? Are you, Susa?

[Tomasso *meantime at the back has set down his organ against the showcase, and stares at* Susa *with wild, eager, large eyes.*]

HARRY. Are you angry, Susa?

TOMASSO. [*Under his breath.*] Susa,—oh!

HARRY. Susa, it wasn't my fault.

SUSA. Oh, basta, basta, it's a lie!

FRITZ. Ach Gott, dese lovers and loveresses! und dis lofe! Gif me my ofen and der furnace for mine! Come, come, don't you be scrappin' —I've got a nice supper for you—all hot.

TOMASSO. [*At the back, stretching out his hands to her and speaking to himself.*] Susa, Susa, Susa!

HARRY. [*By the table on the right.*] Come, Susa, you're wrong! [*She stamps her foot.*] Come, let's eat a bite. All right, Fritz, let's have your feast.

[SUSA *stands with her back to him, without moving.* TOMASSO *at the back looks steadily at* HARRY, *studying him from head to foot, then at himself; back to* HARRY, *then at himself again, and down at his crippled leg; and shakes his head.*]

HARRY. [*Reminding him.*] Fritz——

FRITZ. [*Going out.*] All rightsky, zwei minute!

[FRITZ *goes out.* TOMASSO *puts on his hat and walks over toward the organ.*]

SUSA. I won't eat any supper!

HARRY. Why, Susa, you ain't really mad, are you? Oh, come now, honest, I said I'd wait here.

SUSA. It's a lie—you dodged me—you lie to me—oh, I hate you!

[FRITZ *comes in with a tray of plates.*]

FRITZ. All rightsky—waffles, crab gumbo a la—[SUSA *moves toward the door.*] Hello, where you goin'? Ain't you goin' to eat anythink?

SUSA. I'm going home.

HARRY. Susa, you don't mean it! Then I'll go too.

SUSA. No, sacramento, mai—never—e senta, senta, Harry, listen! Don't you come near me again—don't touch me—or—or I'll kill you, briconaccio—let me be! [*She thrusts him aside and starts toward the door.*]

FRITZ. Susa.

HARRY. Susa——

TOMASSO. No, no! [*He moves quickly in front of her and stands across the door, his hat still down over his eyes.*] No, no, you musta not go. You too quicka——

SUSA. Che, who are you to stop me? Let me pass!

TOMASSO. You are too quicka—there's no

mucha love in dis world—don'ta throw it away—
don't throw it away. Pardone—be gentile——

SUSA. I'll show you how to move!

TOMASSO. [*His manner gathering force as he
stops her with his hand outstretched.*] Aspetti,
wait, waita, wait till you hear——

SUSA. Hear what? Fritz, he is crazy!

TOMASSO. There was a man in my country—
Italia—who loved a woman,—anda she loved him.
And one other personne made lies to them. And
she taka and crede the lies—and leave him and
go to America—epoi—and so—dey lose each
oder.

FRITZ. Why man——!

[SUSA *comes down nearer the table on the
right and stands looking into space, clasping
and unclasping her hands. Harry watches
her anxiously.*]

FRITZ. [*Speaking low to* TOMASSO.] Why,
man, I see, I see—take her—speak!

[TOMASSO *looks at Harry, then at himself;
then points to his crippled leg, and shakes
his head.*]

FRITZ. Fight for your rights—speak up!

TOMASSO. Shh! Hush, signore, hush!

SUSA. [*Raising her head.*] Well?—che ha

fatto? What did he do? What dida that man do?

Tomasso. What do? She go to America, and he cry and cry for her, but never, never found—

Susa. And then?

Tomasso. And then the fever take him and mucha dolore, trouble——

Susa. [*Excitedly.*] And did he follow her?

Tomasso. Si, when he was well again, long time after—to America.

Susa. And found?

Tomasso. [*Slowly.*] And never found.

[Fritz *makes an impatient step forward.*]

Susa. [*Whispering as to herself.*] Ah, never! Madonna!

Tomasso. But if she hadna been so quicka, so fast, so angry—dey had not lost each oder.

Susa. No, maybe not. [*Facing him.*] What was his name?

Tomasso. Tomasso.

[Fritz *and* Harry *look at each other, but remain as they were standing.*]

Susa. [*Taking a step toward him.*] Tomasso?

Tomasso. Si, Tomasso.

Susa. How did you know? Let me see your face—your voice is—oh, are you Tomasso? Have you followed me thena, all this way? Oh, tell me!

TOMASSO. I speaka to make you not leave your man, there——

SUSA. But you, but you, what is your name?

TOMASSO. [*Slowly, with a great effort.*] My name? Luigi—is my name.

[HARRY *and* FRITZ *look suddenly at one another, but seem unable to act.* SUSA *does not recognize* TOMASSO.]

HARRY. Why, why, you will not——?

TOMASSO. [*In a firm voice.*] Luigi.

SUSA. But—how did you know the storia?

TOMASSO. How did I know? I saw it in the play at—Pisa.

SUSA. [*Leaning against the table.*] Ah Dio, I was a fool to think that! I mus' have known— Tomasso, my Tomasso was straight and strong— not [*Looking at Tomasso.*] not——

FRITZ. Oh, Susa!

TOMASSO. Not broke like me, eh? No, not like dis me. Allora—I go. Ricorda, remember the storia!

FRITZ. Stay, stay. Tomas—old chap—and take some zupper wid me—free—I infite you!

TOMASSO. No, I will not eat. I am a little sicka today. I think I'll just taka the bread.

[SUSA *stands on the right, looking at the floor,
struggling to master herself.* TOMASSO
*raises his hat from his face and takes one
long look at her. Then he goes back and
puts the strap over his shoulder; and then
leans suddenly against the organ and buries
his face in his arms.*]

FRITZ. Hey, kiddo!

TOMASSO. [*Rousing gaily and striking up the
waltz.*] Si, si, addio! Where's Gigia? Goodabye—[*Outside.*]—goodabye!

SUSA. Goodbye—Luigi.

[*The organ plays farther and farther away.*]

FRITZ. Ach, his brod!

[*He takes up the bread that* TOMASSO *has left
and starts after him, stops, puts the bread
back on the showcase, and without turning
wipes his eyes on his sleeve.*]

SUSA. Harry——

HARRY. Yes?

SUSA. Perdonnami—I'm sorry.

[*She gives him her hand. The strains of the
waltz die away in a far-off street.*]

CURTAIN

MADRETTA

MADRETTA

SIMON, *a foreman on the levee.*
JEAN MARI, *a Creole, seller of lottery tickets.*
NANI, *a Creole, wife of Simon.*
[*The scene is on the levee in Mississippi, below Greenville. The house is very near the
river. A shack room, with a door on the
left at the back. By the door is a keg covered with scalloped green paper. Above
it is a chromo of the Madonna of the Chair,
and a crucifix; on it are some paper flowers
and a candle in a bottle.*
*To the middle right is the bed, in a diagonal
position. Still further to the right is a door
or window hung with a red and drab curtain. By the left wall is a box with a poor
mirror and a few household articles. When
the curtain rises, Nani is standing in a de-
jected attitude on the step just outside the
doorway. She has a flower in her hand,
which she throws away before entering. She
draws a box from under the bed, and takes
out some baby toys.*]

27

NANI. [*Looking at the toys.*] Pierre—petit
Pierre—mamie. [*She puts the toys back, sits in
the low chair and sings.*] Rockabye, baby, in the
tree tops, When the wind blows, the cradle, the
cradle—[*She is choked with sobs.*] Ah, non,
non! Ca ne me fait rien—il me faut oublier.
[*Sings.*] Il pleut, bergère—non, I cannot—[*She
lights the candle in front of the crucifix and
picture.*] Madonna, Madonna, hear me, Madonna—you had a child too——

[*In the distance is heard* JEAN MARI'S *voice
singing gaily.* MADRETTA *hears. She looks
quickly at the crucifix, then listens to the
nearing voice. She presses her hands to her
breast. Her eyes are wide with excitement.*]

NANI. O Jesus,—Jean Mari!

[*She extinguishes the candle, and runs out.
In a moment she returns with* JEAN MARI.
She has the flower in her hair now. JEAN
MARI *carries a pink paper in his hand.*]

JEAN MARI. And you hear me sing?

NANI. Yais, oh, yais, it is our song you were
singing,—Il pleut bergère—Simon, my man, my
husband, he never sings.

JEAN MARI. Never sing, not he, he is the
Yankee, he works.

NANI. Yais, Simon works, does he. At home

we never worked. Not much we worked, yais.
But I think I sing more then maybe than now.

JEAN MARI. New Orleans?

NANI. Oui, Nouvelle Orleans, yais, before I
married Simon.

JEAN MARI. Oh, Nani, if I had found you
then!

NANI. Before, yais, before. I would not have
cried so much then, because I might have stayed
in Nouvelle Orleans.

JEAN MARI. Yes, you might have stayed in
New Orleans. We'd have been happy, Nani.

NANI. Think so,—yais, before, before, before
I married Simon—and the baby was born, and
we came here, and this swamp killed my child—
my lil Pierre——

JEAN MARI. Non, non——

NANI. And then I cry toujours, always. I
can no thing but crying. And Simon, the
man, he maybe forget soon—I don't know, he
say so lil bit, so lil bit, Simon. He say "Madretta," that means lil mother you know, he
named me that from what the Dagoes say, "Madretta you cry your heart out, it's na good, leave
the cryin."

JEAN MARI. But I was sorry for you.

NANI. Yais, and sat with me in the long daytime when Simon was gone to work with the men up yonder. You love me, hey?

JEAN MARI. Love you? Ah Nani! I have brought you these bijoux, Nani. [*He takes out a string of coral beads. She puts them on with delight.*] Love you, Nani——

NANI. But we must not talk that. Simon, he never talks of you.

JEAN MARI. Simon he likes me not.

NANI. I don't know—maybe—Simon, I think he is sick a lil. But he say nothing. He works hard and saves the money.

JEAN MARI. Miser—diable——

NANI. I don't know 'bout that. He never beats me about the money as my father he used to do. Ah, non, ciel—[*She catches sight of herself in the glass.*] The flower is pretty, jolie——

JEAN MARI. Pretty on Nani, yes.

NANI. Yais, am I pretty? I don't know. Simon told me so before we were married. Jolie? Who is here to say that? No one is ever in the swamp to look at me. Here's nothing, nothing but the trees and the wind they are all. The wind in the trees makes me afraid, and when I hear the birds, when I hear them I cry for my baby.

JEAN MARI. Simon could tell you if he would. Do you love him, Nani?

NANI. I don't know, ciel! He is most kind, and never quarrels. He brought me the cross there, see, over the Blessed Virgin. Le's not talk 'bout that. What is the papier, Jean Mari?

JEAN MARI. The steamer, Kate Adams.

NANI. Where?

JEAN MARI. New Orleans.

NANI. Oh, non—Nouvelle Orleans—when?

JEAN MARI. In one hour. [*Looking at watch.*] Ten o'clock it says.

[*She goes to the door and looks out. Raises one hand, and drops it.*]

JEAN MARI. Nani——

NANI. Yais, Jean Mari.

JEAN MARI. New Orleans, Nani.

NANI. Yais, I understand—Nouvelle Orleans.

JEAN MARI. Where you cry to go, Nani, and Simon will not go.

NANI. Yais, *he* will not go, Simon.

JEAN MARI. Nani——

NANI. Yais——

JEAN MARI. [*Starting toward her.*] I will take you, Nani! I will take you. I love you, Nani, more than your wooden Yankee does.

NANI. [*Struggling.*] Non, Jean Mari, ah, non——

JEAN MARI. Mais oui, but yes! New Orleans —see I have the money here.

NANI. Eh bien——

JEAN MARI. The children and the music in the street—the blessed mass, we 'll sing all day —what is there here; Nani?

NANI. Here?

JEAN MARI. Oui, yes, here?

NANI. Simon, he is here.

JEAN MARI. Ah, the Yankee, he is one ox.

NANI. He has been kind to me, maybe——

JEAN MARI. Nani, the girls and boys, Suzanne and Desirée, and the piano in the park at night. You can do it all, quick——

NANI. He might come back here before the hour, might Simon. He will kill me!

JEAN MARI. He comes not ever back till night. You know the overflow, the levee needs him,——

NANI. The overflow?

JEAN MARI. Yes, he must be with the levee, or what may happen! He never comes back till dark—he *shall* not come. [*She is irresolute.*] He will never find you in the city, he will not search.

NANI. Maybe he will not search—I don't know,—maybe he will be glad if I go. I go with you,—to Nouvelle Orleans—[*He starts toward her again.*] Non, non, Jean Mari, leave me to fix. Don't touch me. Leave me to fix.

JEAN MARI. Not long.

NANI. Not long, yais. [*He goes out. She closes the door, and stands a moment wide-eyed.*] Ah, Nouvelle Orleans, Nouvelle Orleans! [*Sets frantically about her packing.*]

[*Presently a halloa is heard in the direction of the river. Then a pistol shot, followed by another. NANI starts up in terror. SIMON stumbles into the door, and leans against the wall.*]

NANI. [*Running to fasten the door.*] Simon!

SIMON. Nani, quick.

NANI. Simon, are you hurt?

[*He takes his hand from within his coat, and holds it palm outward. It is covered with blood.*]

NANI. Who? Who?

SIMON. Oh, I don't know. It's no matter who.

NANI. O God!

SIMON. Help me, Madretta, to the bed. [*He*

lies with his head to the foot.] Little Madretta —oh, give me some wine, woman! [*She gives him wine.*]

NANI. Get the doctor! Let me go for the doctor!

SIMON. No, no, no, you could not get him here in time—sit by me, Madretta.

NANI. You bleed?

SIMON. Inside I think—in my breast here. It trickles and strangles sort o'. It is not long.

NANI. [*Giving him more wine.*] You come home soon today.

SIMON. Yes, I ran all——

NANI. Ran?

SIMON. Listen, Madretta—let me speak while I can. That lottery fellow, Jean Mari, has been selling liquor to the men—he's the cause of all this——

NANI. Are you easy now, lying so?

SIMON. Raise my head—now.

NANI. Oui, so.

SIMON. The levee is broke above—they say it will sweep all this place away. I could hear it comin' when I started. They say there is a boat —I came to save you——

NANI. Yais, to save me——

SIMON. Yes, to save you. And when I got

to the cattle-pen out there, somebody called and
then shot. [*Coughs blood.*]

NANI. [*Rising.*] Yais, to save me, Simon.
Maybe you love me then.

SIMON. Love you, oh, Madretta——

NANI. You never say so.

SIMON. Don't you know me yet? I never
say such things, Madretta.

[*She falls on her knees by the bed.*]

NANI. Don' die! See, it do not bleed now!

SIMON. In here, in here—I feel it settling.
[*He puts his arm about her neck.*] Little
Madretta, Nani—I'm so sleepy—maybe I'd bet-
ter go to sleep a bit.

[*He dozes. She stands on her knees and looks
at him. The whistle of a steamboat is heard in
the distance. Simon talks in a sort of delirium.*]
My little son, and little Madretta—that's sweet,
little mother—my lil son is dead—but I must not
cry—that would make it harder for Nani. I—I
can grieve when I am working in the day. We
must save money. If I have enough money to
leave this damned swamp New Year, maybe in
the spring that levee will burst and ruin us—
New Year. New Year we'll go. I'll not tell her
—though. Because if we didn't really go—why
—. Nani, are you there?

NANI. Yais, yais.

SIMON. [*Changing his tone.*] It's no use to cry, woman. It won't bring the baby back, nor put us in New Orleans. [*Changes tone again.*] There,—poor lil mother! Nani, where are the candles, Nani? It's dark in this corner. Nani!

NANI. Yais——

SIMON. Madretta, light the candles.

NANI. [*Lighting the candles in a blind sort of fashion.*] Now you see, do you?

SIMON. A little. [*He is silent a while, suddenly sits up.*] Here, baby, come here. Call him, Madretta! He is afraid of the blood. Pierre! Call him, mother.

NANI. [*Following his gaze, numbly.*] Where? [*She comes to herself, and drops back into her seat.*] Hush, Simon, hush!

[*He lies back.*]

SIMON. Goodnight, baby Pierre. Madretta—

NANI. I hear you—yais——

SIMON. Madretta, don' leave me,—you are all I have left—you are all I have. Reach me your hand. It's night now, and I am tired. [*He seems to sleep.*]

NANI. Yais, I'm here, Simon. I won't leave you—I won't, Simon.

[*There comes a knock at the door, and* JEAN
MARI'S *voice outside.*]

JEAN MARI. [*Outside.*] Nani—Nani——
                [*No answer.*]

JEAN MARI. [*Knocking.*] Nani — come,
Nani——

NANI. Jean Mari——

JEAN MARI. I shot him to keep him away.
He's in the woods somewhere. You are safe,
open the door.

NANI. Open the door——
                [*The whistle is heard.*]

JEAN MARI. [*Shaking door.*] Nani, Nani—
the boat is stopping up yonder. We'll be home
tomorrow—in New Orleans.

NANI. Nouvelle Orleans.

[*She looks at* SIMON *who seems to be dead.
    She is afraid of him. She rises. She starts
    toward the door, passing her open hand
    along the wall, as if half blind.*]

JEAN MARI. Nani—quick—Nani——

NANI. I hear you.

[*Suddenly her blind hand strikes the crucifix,
    which falls before her. She recoils from it
    in terror. The boat whistles twice. Bells.*]

JEAN MARI. Nani, don't be afraid, come——

[*Bells. She takes two steps toward the door,
then a step back toward the bed.* SIMON
stirs and tries to raise his head.]

SIMON. Madretta, are you there? You're all
I have, Madretta——

[JEAN MARI *shakes the door.*]

SIMON. Madretta——

[*She stands by the bed. Her eyes blaze and
her bosom heaves.*]

NANI. Yais, Simon.

JEAN MARI. [*Outside.*] Will you come, Nani?
Damn you, are you coming or not?

[*Her hand at her breast finds the beads. She
tears them from her throat and hurls them
at the door. The beads rattle over the
boards.*]

NANI. Non, non, I will not.

SIMON. Madretta——

[*The whistle and the bells are farther off. The
noise of the flood, accompanied by the crack-
ing of the timber, grows gradually louder.*]

NANI. Simon, Simon. [*Shaking him.*] Simon,
the overflow!

SIMON. [*Fretful and almost asleep.*] Madretta——

[*She comes back to the bed, walking like a*

stunned thing, and falls on her knees by him.]

SIMON. [*Feeling for her hand.*]   Little Madretta——

NANI.   I am with you.
          [*The flood roars outside.*]

CURTAIN

THE STAR IN THE TREES

To

Orlando Rouland

THE STAR IN THE TREES

ASTORRI.
LYANE, *his sister.*
DAPHNE.
SYRINX.
THE NIGHT WIND.
THE QUEEN OF FAERIE.
THE VOICE OF THE WATER.
THE DEW.
THE SEVEN SHADOWS.
THE VOICE IN THE ASPEN TREE.
ECHO.

*Scene.—A secret wood. To the front right is
a fountain thick set about with reeds and
water flags. To the left at the back the* DEW
lies asleep on the grass.

*On the left stands a laurel tree, slim and tall;
in the centre at the back an aspen tree.
Shadows nestle beneath the trees. There is
a faint twilight over the scene.*

ASTORRI *enters at the back, carrying a book,
and comes down toward the front.*

45

LYANE.   [*Outside.*]

Astorri!

ASTORRI.

Aye, Lyane——

LYANE.

Wilt thou leave me?

ASTORRI.

Nay, little sister, I do wait.   Lyane,
Lyane, art thou not weary?

LYANE.   [*Enters.*]

Aye, weary are my feet but not my heart.
I will fare with thee to the happy wood.

ASTORRI.

Yea, let us go.   For in my dreams have I
Seen heavy grief and thick shapes crowding on,
And some unrest that would unnerve my heart.
To me the world is all of shadowy omens;
And never do I see a falling star
That underneath the ground sinks into night,
But that I mark the setting stars of fate;—

LYANE.

Further, yet further, have we dreamed the while.

ASTORRI.

Aye, far away the vision of a song
Brought to mine ear a secret wood, and showed

A covert place of freedom from the strife.
Let us still seek.

LYANE.

Hast thou the book?

ASTORRI.

Aye, here.

LYANE.

How wilt thou know the place?

ASTORRI.

Knowest thou not yet?   A yellow stone is there,
A laurel tree, a fountain rimmed with green,
And silence—and in the pool——

LYANE.

Brother Astorri, look thou!

ASTORRI.

What?

LYANE.

Beside thee, look!—a little fountain—see—
And there, the stone!

ASTORRI.

Keep us, O Queen of Faerie, from deceit!
The fountain and the stone—Lyane, Lyane,
Is 't not a laurel there?

LYANE.

Aye, haply, then will I break and see.

ASTORRI.

Nay, break it not, Lyane! Do thou not mar
The children of the wood; who knoweth when
Within the leafy breast doth lie some grief,
Some spirit frail and old unhappiness—
Break thou it not!

LYANE.

It is a laurel by the leaf.

ASTORRI.

Laurel?

LYANE.

What further sayeth the book?

ASTORRI.

Thou shalt unto a fountain in the wood,
And rosemary and rue shalt put therein,
And one frail primrose from the passing spring;
And there thy falling tears shall show thee solace.

LYANE.

I do remember me.

ASTORRI.

Hast thou the flowers ready?

LYANE.

Aye, near my heart they lie.

[*She takes from her bosom the flowers and
drops them one by one into the pool as she
speaks.*]

ASTORRI.

Rosemary from the garden of the heart,
And rue that grows where sadness hath her seat,
And primroses that smile and die too soon.

LYANE.

Read on, yet how hast read in darkness?

ASTORRI.

My heart hath read, Lyane—and now, behold
How still the water lies, like sleep.

[*They kneel above the pool and watch.*]

ASTORRI.

Seest thou naught?

LYANE.

Alas, naught! Brother, my heart faileth.

ASTORRI.

Weep not. I see the ripple of thy tear,
And now another falls,—weep not, dear child,—
[*A light flashes through the water of the pool.*]
Lo, mark thee, comes a light!—thou mindst the
     book,
It is thy falling tears that loosed the spell.

LYANE.

Look, look, Astorri, where she sitteth there,
Braiding her locks with pearls, the water sprite,
The silver fishes round her feet—hark thou—!

[*The sound of the nymph singing comes from
the water of the pool.*]

THE WATER NYMPH'S FOREST SONG

Alas, I hear their voices call,
Come sad and sweet, come sweet and sad,
And woe is me, poor water thrall,
Who mourn the joy that once I had.
Lo, where they dwell within the trees,
All mournfully, all mournfully,
Who drinketh of this flood he sees
Their misery, their misery.
Weladay!

ASTORRI.

Of whom sang she?

LYANE.

Of them that hidden dwell in wretchedness
Within the mystic leafage of the wood.

ASTORRI.

What said the song?

LYANE.

That if thou drinkest there thou mayest hear
The secret of the place.

ASTORRI.

Then will I drink.

LYANE.

Stay, Brother, stay! Art thou not half adread
Of some enchantment in the cup?

ASTORRI.

Yet will I drink.
    [*He dips his hand into the pool and drinks.*]

LYANE.

Alas, Astorri!

ASTORRI.

Hist!

LYANE.

What is it?

ASTORRI.

Dost thou hear a song? And now another—
    drink,
Drink quickly! [*He gives her water with his
    hands rounded together.*]

LYANE.

Listen, oh, listen!
    [*The sound of sighing comes from the trees
    of the wood, the singing of wind, and a low
    music from the grass. The voice of the
    nymph is heard farther away.*]

ASTORRI.

I see the stars blown through the sky like
    sparks

From watchfires on the hills!
[*The place grows gradually lighter. Daphne
    appears from the laurel. The* SHADOWS *stir
    in their haunts, and* DEW *awakens on the
    grass.*]

LYANE.

Look, look, Astorri, where she lies, more fresh
Than April showers at the dawn. Speak,
Who art thou?

DEW.

Dew am I. I am Dew, daughter of Twilight
And sister of the Morning.

ASTORRI.

Knowest thou the secret of this place, oh say?

DEW.

I know the fresh heart of the woodland green,—
To wake at morn with sunlight in mine eyes,
And through the day to follow shadowy glades
Till twilight calls me to the fields again.

LYANE.

Will it be ever thus? Is it enough?

DEW.

Enough to lie in verdurous happiness,
And be playfellow to the violet,
And hawthorn whose white petals kiss my face.

LYANE.

Can that be all of life, this dew-fed joy?

THE VOICE OF ECHO.

Alas, alas!

ASTORRI.

Hist!

DEW.

Behold my leader cometh, the Night Wind!

[THE NIGHT WIND *enters.* *She is clothed in* *silver, flecked with stars and flowers and* *blown leaves.*]

LYANE.

I smell the perfume of her hair.

THE VOICE OF ECHO.

Alas, alas! Woe is my heart!

LYANE.

Ah me, who waileth so in sorrow?

THE VOICE OF ECHO.

Echo am I, who dwell amid the glooms.
I loved the youth who turned in scorn from me,
And through the weary years I call and call,
And sigh myself into a voice—alas,
Forever and forever.

LYANE.

Alas, Night Wind, may'st thou not comfort her?

THE NIGHT WIND.

Echo, Echo, thou child of misery,
Lo, have I borne thy sorrow round the world,
And unto men whose hearts are ashes, told
The burden of thy sadness and thy love.

THE VOICE OF ECHO.

If I might but return to flesh again,
Leaving this deathless grief, and die and pass,
As women do whom love hath mocked—alas—
  [*The voices of the wood increase.*]

ASTORRI.

How all the wood with wailing cries! And thou,
Frail Maiden in thy laurel, sure thy voice
Is sweet with ancient sorrow, who art thou?

DAPHNE.

Once dwelt I in the vales of Arcady,
And fed at morn the myrtles with bright dew,
And homeward led my quiet flock at even—

LYANE.

What then hath changed thee?

DAPHNE.

Chaste Dian hid me in the laurel's heart
When I sought refuge from his fierce desire,
Apollo of the shining head. Ah, shame,
Still hear I those hot words—*Stay, Daphne,
    stay!*—

Still feel the burning wind upon my face,
And creeping o'er my skin the cruel bark,
And my bright hair to waving leafage sprung.

ASTORRI.

Then Daphne art thou!

DAPHNE.

Even so, Daphne.

LYANE.

Alas, poor child!

DAPHNE.

Far, far from life and human kind I dwell,
A deathless sorrow in a deathless youth;
Would I had died!

LYANE.

Deathless seem all the sorrows of this place;
I never thought to meet such agony
Hidden within the quiet wood.

ASTORRI.

I hear even the dead crying in the sod.

LYANE.

Listen, oh, listen, at the fluted reeds
Uttering sweet voices in their twilight bed,
To charm the ancient dusk of quietness.

    [*A song like the notes of a flute is heard near
      by the pool.* SYRINX *rises among the reeds.*]

ASTORRI.

Say, Maiden, who art thou, with the claspéd
    hands
And most sad burthen, who art thou?

LYANE.

Thy most sad song like lonely shepherd's pipe.
    [SYRINX *disappears among the reeds again,
    and the flute notes wail and grow softer and
    softer.*]

ASTORRI.

Gone like a star in water!

LYANE.

Alas, who is she?

DAPHNE.

Syrinx is she, whom cruel Pan desired,
And Dian changéd into humble reeds
Whose wail alone repaid his mad embraces.

ASTORRI.

Even the river marge unto the water tells
Its tale of sorrow—

LYANE.

Alas, poor Syrinx, what is spring to thee,
The flowering banks and petals on the grass,
And warm young southwind stirring mid the
    reeds?
All the sweet season mendeth not thy grief!

THE NIGHT WIND.

Shall we have naught but woe? Surely I hear
Enough of sadness in my wandering,
Enough of crying hearts and fevered lips—
Come, shall we not sing? What, Shadows, ho!
Little brown mischiefs in your shady clefts,
Out, out and dance before your master wind!

[THE SEVEN SHADOWS *start from under the
boughs, singing and joining in a dance.*]

SHADOW SONG.

Heigho, under the bough,
Flicker and shimmer and dance and sing!
Heigho, thou leafy tree,
Rustle and flutter and sway and swing!
Dance, Sister Shadows, and laughter bring,
Heigho, happy be!

[*A horn is wound far off. The* SHADOWS
*break their dance and flit back to their
nestling places.*]

ASTORRI.

What voice is that whose charméd minstrelsy
Sends magic and enchantment through the place,
Stilling the very shadows of the wood?

THE NIGHT WIND.

It is the Elfland Horn

ASTORRI.

Look, look, Lyane, where lo, one cometh!

LYANE.

Astorri, is she not fair?

ASTORRI.

Ah, gentle Night Wind, say, who is it cometh?
Her brow is ivy bound, her step is free,
Her robe like starlight scattered over mist!

LYANE.

Her eyes are haunted.

[THE QUEEN OF FAERIE *enters*.]

THE NIGHT WIND.

The Queen of Faerie!

ASTORRI.

Surely our search is ended!

THE QUEEN OF FAERIE.

Night Wind, go wake yon Dew that dreaming
lies.
On the high hills my people are athirst,
The upland grass is dry and sorrowful.

THE NIGHT WIND.

Arise and hasten, the hills await thy feet.

DEW.

Under the stars my fingers scatter life,

And ere the hedgerow bird his matin sings,
I shall await thee at the green wayside.

    [THE DEW *goes out, and* THE NIGHT WIND
    follows her, scattering flowers and leaves
    as she goes.]

THE QUEEN OF FAERIE.

Who are ye and what seek ye here?

ASTORRI.

Astorri I, and this, Lyane, my sister.
Who seek the woodland's heart and its deep
    silence.
We were aghast of life, and from the ills
That loomed before, we turned our steps away
And sought the land of faery.

ECHO.

Alas, this wretched land!

THE VOICE FROM THE WATER.

Ah, realm of endless doom!

ASTORRI.

Teach us to be as thou and thine, and show
How we may shun the garish highway.

THE QUEEN OF FAERIE.

The realm of faerie mocks the world's delight;
Man's life is but a dewdrop on a leaf
That quivers with the wind. But here we dwell

In an eternity of verdant bliss;
And children of the moon and starlight be,
Of flitting shadows and the sylvan streams.
The loves of men, their travail and their woe,
Break not the green veil of our vision; pain
Toucheth us not, death cometh not to us,
And all the wailing of the world goes by
As idle wind; nor are our hearts more touched
Than are the hardy fibres of the trees.

LYANE.

Can this be happiness, think you?

ASTORRI.

I know not if it be, I only know
In it there are no terrors and no dooms
But armor against pain. Tell us, O Queen,
How we may come to thee!

LYANE.

Wilt thou forget thy people and thy blood
And change thy heart, Astorri?

ASTORRI.

I would forget the sorrow!

THE QUEEN OF FAERIE.

Dost thou not hear the horns of elfland blowing?

ASTORRI.

Doth not their magic haunt the very leaves,

Unto the hills and dingles calling me?

LYANE.

Alas, the light within thine eyes, dear brother,
Thine eyes are cold and see me not!

THE QUEEN OF FAERIE.

If thou wouldst come unto forgetfulness,
To leave the weary folk and live as we,
Bind thy young brows with ivy and slit thine
eyes,
That thou mayest think and see as doon the
faerie.

LYANE.

Alas, what wilt thou have him do?

ASTORRI.

If I should follow then?

THE QUEEN OF FAERIE.

Thou shalt forget the world of time and grief,
And tree and star shall all thy brethren be.
Shadow and sunlight will encircle thee
With an unceasing dance of happy life,
Thou shalt have hillside dreams and moonlit
sleep,
And sweet oblivious twilight in thy soul.

ASTORRI.

I will go with thee!

LYANE.

Astorri! Brother!

THE QUEEN OF FAERIE.

Beneath the haunted oak shalt lie and hear
The reedy brook go singing in the wind,
And mark the murmuring world grow less and
    less.

ASTORRI.

Let it be now, I pray thee!

THE QUEEN OF FAERIE.

Then must I blind thine eyes of all the past.

LYANE.

Give not thine eyes, O Brother!

THE QUEEN OF FAERIE.

And nevermore shall fall a tear from them.

ASTORRI.

Quickly I pray thee, show the land of faerie!
  [THE QUEEN OF FAERIE *takes out a slim dag-*
    ger to slit his eyes.]

LYANE.

Save him, O God, show him some sign and save!
Is all the wood unto enchantment yielded?
A sign, a sign—!
  [*Darkness comes suddenly over the wood.*
    With sharp cries DAPHNE *flees to her prison*

again. In the aspen tree at the back, a burning cross appears, high up among the leaves. ASTORRI *drops on his knees before the tree,* LYANE *beside him.* THE QUEEN OF FAERIE *has vanished.*]

ASTORRI.

Whither, whither, O Queen? Where is Echo?

DAPHNE.

[*From the laurel.*] Alas, a greater woe than mine is here!

ECHO.

Alas, I am as naught before this pain!

THE VOICE FROM THE ASPEN TREE.

Behold the cross whose sorrow blessed the world!
Turn thou unto that passion and be whole.

LYANE.

Lo, how still the wood, the anguish dies!

THE VOICE FROM THE ASPEN TREE.

To His immortal pain theirs is as smoke.
These thou hast seen are single agonies,
Of men and maidens frail, whose loved delight
Turned fire upon their lips and left them seared.
They suffered for themselves, but He for all;
His large desire included all of man,
And in His eye the vision of the race,
And in His heart the tears of all the world!

ASTORRI.
Hither we came to seek out happiness
And dim oblivion from life and grief,
What may we do?

THE VOICE FROM THE ASPEN TREE.
Turn back, turn back again unto thy life,
And strive thou not to leave the earthly road;
And thou shalt come at last unto thy kingdom;
And in kind eyes thou shalt lay down thy care,
And by thy fellow's side shalt find thy rest,
And in thy fellow's love thy land of faery.
[The arms of the cross dwindle to a star.]
Follow the star!

ASTORRI.
Hail star of the world!

LYANE.
Hail, our brother, Christ!
*[The star appears farther away, on the path
by which ASTORRI and LYANE entered. They
rise from their knees and begin to follow it.]*

THE VOICES OF THE WIND AND WOOD.
Hail Star of the World,
Hail our brother Christ!
*[The star appears and reappears, further and
further off, along the path; ASTORRI and
LYANE disappear, following its lead.]*

THE VOICES.
[*Farther away, and following the star.*]
Hail, Star of the world,
Hail, our brother Christ!
Hail, Hail!
[*Darkness falls in the wood.*]

THE TWILIGHT SAINT

To

Sarah and Frances Starks

THE TWILIGHT SAINT

GUIDO, *the husband, a young poet.*
LISETTA, *his wife.*
PIA, *a neighbor woman.*
ST. FRANCIS OF ASSISI.
In the year 1215 A. D.

SCENE.—*A room in* GUIDO'S *house, on a hillside near Bevagna. It is a poor apartment
clumsily kept. On the left near the front
is a bed; on the floor by the bed lie scattered
pages of manuscript. A table littered with
manuscripts and crockery stands against the
wall to the right of the door. On the right
to the front is a big fireplace with copper
and brass vessels. A bench sits by the fireplace and several stools about the room. On
the stone flags two sheepskins are spread.
Through the door rises the slope of a hill,
green with spring and starred with flowers.
A stream is visible through the grass and
the drowsy sound of the water fills the air.
The late yellow sunlight falls through a*

*window over the bed and floods the hillside
without.*
LISETTA *lies on the bed, still, her eyes closed.*
PIA *sits on the ingle bench, shelling peas.*
GUIDO *sits at the table, his face to the wall,
his chin on his palm.*

PIA.

Guido, Guido, thou hast not spoke this hour,
Nor read one word nor written aught.   Dear
Lord,
The lion on the palace at Assisi
Sits not more still in stone.   Guido, look thou.

GUIDO.

[*Turning round without looking at her.*]
Yes, old Pia, good neighbor.

PIA.

Yes, old Pia! Guido, grieve not o'ermuch,
Lisetta will be well before the spring
Comes round again.

GUIDO.

Yes, she will mend belike; 'tis not of her.
There is much else, O Pia! here am I
Shut in this house from month to month a nurse.
Here lies she sick, this child, and may not stir;
And I, lacking due means to hire, must serve
The house, while my best self, my soul, my art,

Do rust. My soul is scorched with holy thirst,
My temples throb, my veins run fire; but yet,
For all my dim distress and vague desire,
No word written, no single song, no verse—
O blessed God!—stifled with creature needs,
And hard necessity about my throat!

PIA.

Thy corner is too hot, the glaring sun
Is yet upon the wall.

GUIDO.

'Tis not that sun that maddens me, O Pia!
Can you not see me shrunk? Have you not
    heard
That other Guido of Perugia
How he is grown? How lately at the feast
That Ugolino the great cardinal
Spread at Assisi Easter night, Guido
Read certain of his verses and declaimed
Pages of cursed sonnets to the guests.

PIA.

Young Guido of Perugia, thy friend?

GUIDO.

Yea. And when he ended, came the Duke
Down from his dais to kiss that Guido's hand
Humbly, and said that poesy was king.

PIA.

Madonna, kissed by the Duke!

GUIDO.

And I, oh God, I might have honor too,
Could I but leave this prison where I drudge.

PIA.

Speak low, her sleep is light. Her road is hard
As well as thine. For all this year, since thou
Didst bring her from Rieto here to us,
Hath she lain on her bed, broken with pain,
This child that is thy wife and loveth thee.

GUIDO.

Aye, yes, 'tis true, she loveth me, she loveth me,
And I love her. 'Tis worse—add grief to care,
And Poesy fares worse.

PIA.

And she is grown most pale and still of late.

GUIDO.

Look, Pia, how she lieth there like death,
That far-off patience on her face. Now, now,
Surely I needs must make a song! And yet
I may not; ashes and floor-sweeping clog
My soul within me.

PIA.

Nay, let thy poems pass. Look thou, how pale!

Dear Lord, how blue her little veins do shine!

GUIDO.

Thou art most kind, good neighbor, to come here
Helping our house. But thou knowest not, nor
      canst,
The poet's realm. For in my soul I hear
A bell summoning me always—

PIA.

If I should stew in milk the peas, maybe—
Dost think the child would eat of it?

GUIDO.

Thy world is not my world. I will go out
Alone.

PIA.

I have an hour yet.

GUIDO.

Be sure I will return unto my chores,
Mine is a short tether.

  [*He goes out.* LISETTA *on the bed opens her
      eyes.*]

LISETTA.

Pia.

PIA.

Yes, dear child.

LISETTA.

Turn thou my pillow, I am stifled.

PIA.

There.   Thou hast slept well?

LISETTA.

I have not slept.

PIA.

Holy Virgin, thou hast not slept?

LISETTA.

Pia, think you I did not know?   This month
I scarce have slept for thinking on his lot.
I read his fighting soul.   Where are his songs,
The great renown that waited him?   Down,
      down,
Struck by the self-same hand that shattered me.
I listen night on night and hear him moan
In his sleep—

PIA.

It is his love for thee, Lisetta.

LISETTA.

The padre from the village hemmed and said
That God had sent me and my sickness here
For Guido's cross to bear, his scourge.   They
      thought
I slept—

PIA.

Thou hast dreamed this, he loveth thee—

LISETTA.

Yea, loveth me somewhat, but glory more!
And I would have it so. O Mother of God,
When wilt thou send me death?

PIA.

Beware, Lisetta, tempt not God!

LISETTA.

Death is the sister of all them that weep.

PIA.

Child, child, try thou to sleep.

LISETTA.

For thy sake will I try.

PIA.

Hist!

LISETTA.

What, good Pia?

PIA.

Footsteps—a monk!
  [FRANCIS OF ASSISI *stands on the doorstep.*]
Father, come in, the road is hot and weary,
And thou seemst worn and faint.

FRANCIS.

I have not eaten food this day. Hast thou
Somewhat that I may eat?

Pia.

Alas, poor brother, sit thee here.   'Tis bread
And cheese and lentils, eat thy store.   Poor 'tis,
But given in His name.

Francis.

I will eat then and bless thee.

Pia.

Thou takest but a crust.

Francis.

It is enough.   He that doth eat
The bread of life hath little hunger in him.

Pia.

Sit thou and rest, poor soul.

Francis.

Nay, nay, I may not tarry, there is much
To do that waits for me.   My daughter, child,
Thou sleepest not, for all thy lowered lids.
Tears quiver on thy lashes, hast thou pain?

Lisetta.

The tears of women even in dreams may fall,
Good brother.   Wilt thou not bide?

Francis.

I must fare on.

Lisetta.

Aye, aye, the world lies open to thy hand,

But unto me this twelvemonth is a death.
The flesh is dead, and dying lies my soul,
Shrunk like a flower in my fevered hand.
I may not see the stars rise on the hills,
Nor tend the flocks at even, nor rise to do
Aught of the small sweet round of duties owed
To him I love; but lie a burden to him,
Calling on death who heareth not.

FRANCIS.
My life hath shown me words for thee to hear.

LISETTA.
Surely thy life is peace.

FRANCIS.
There is a life larger than life, that dwells
Invisible from all, whose lack alone
Is death.   There in thy soul the stars may rise,
And at the even the gentle thoughts return
To flock the quiet pastures of the mind;
And in the large heart love is all thou owest
For service unto God and thy Beloved.
God's peace I give to you, dear friends.   Farewell.

[*He goes out. *PIA *stands a moment wiping
her eyes, then returns to shelling the peas.
There is a silence for a while.*]

PIA.

Why dost thou look so long upon the door?

LISETTA.

How doth the spring smile on the tender grass!
Meseems the sun is brighter where he stood.

PIA.

'Tis a glaring sun for twilight.

LISETTA.

Nay, nay, 'twill be the gentlest of all eves.
Surely God sent the brother for my need,
To give His peace.

PIA.

Aye, and my old heart ripens at his words
Like apples in the sun.   'Tis a sweet monk.

LISETTA.

Who is he, think you?

PIA.

One of the Little Poor Men, by his brown.
They are too thin these brothers and do lack
Stomach for life. Mark! Oh, 'tis merry now
To see the little beggars from their pods
Popping like schoolboys from their shoes in
        spring!
The season hath been so fine and dry this year
My peas are smaller and must have more work.

Well, well, labor is good, and things made
  scarce
Are better loved.

LISETTA.

Pia, thou art a good woman.

PIA.

Nay, child, make me not cry.   'Tis thy pure
  heart
Deceives thee.   Stubborn I am and full of sloth,
And a wicked heart.

LISETTA.

I would not grieve thee.   Pia, 'twas my love
That sees thy goodness better than thyself.

PIA.

[*Setting the kettle of peas on the coals.*]
Dearie, the sky is at the chimney top.

[*She sings.*]
Firefly, firefly, come from the shadows,
Twilight is falling over the meadows,
Burn, little garden lamps, flicker and shimmer,
Shine, little meadow stars, twinkle and glimmer,
Firefly, firefly, shine, shine!

LISETTA.

Pia.

PIA.

Yes.

LISETTA.

Pia, come near me here. [PIA *kneels by the
    bed.*] Can you not see
How much I love? If I could only speak
To him or he to me, Guido my love!

PIA.

Surely he is beside thee often.

LISETTA.

His hand is near, but not his heart.

PIA.

Nay, nay, child, 'tis his way. He speaks but
    little.

LISETTA.

Aye, tell me not. On winter nights I lay,
Hearing the tree limbs rattle there like hail,
And from the corner eaves the dropping rain
Like big dogs lapping all about—and he
Spoke not to me, but sat beside his taper
And never a line wrote down. Once had I
    words,
Bright dreams that spoke through him, the same
    fire shone
Through both, his songs were mine.

PIA.

Aye, thine—rest thee, rest thee!

LISETTA.

But more his, Pia, more his.

PIA.

Aye, his. Wilt thou not eat the broth?

LISETTA.

Not now, good Pia, 'tis not for food I die.
'Tis not for food.

PIA.

Yet thou must eat.

LISETTA.

Wilt thou not read one song of these to me?

PIA.

Close then thine eyes and rest.

[LISETTA *closes her eyes.* PIA *takes up at ran-*
dom a sheet of the manuscripts. She sighs
a great sigh. Mimics LISETTA'S *voice.*]

PIA.

The Ballad of the Running Water.
O, music locked amid the stones,
Beside the—amid the

LISETTA.

Read on—and thou hast told me day by day
Thou couldst not read.

PIA.

I read by hearing thee from day to day

Repeat the reading.

LISETTA.

Fie! Give me the verses.

[*She takes the paper, but reads without look-
ing at it.*]
*O, music locked amid the stones,
My love hath spoken like to thee,*
Pia, think you—Pia, do you not hear
The mowers and the reapers in the fields
Singing the evening song, and the twilight
pipes?
The twilight is the hour when hearts break!
How many lonely twilights, will there be
Ere God will spare me?

PIA.   [*Kneeling.*]

Hush, child, hush, darling!

[LISETTA *turns her face to the window by the
bed.* PIA *strokes her hand and sings softly.*]
Firefly, firefly, come from the shadows—
Hist! he is coming now, I hear his step
Upon the gravel road. Good night, sweet child,
I'll get me home.

LISETTA.

Pia, goodnight once more.

[GUIDO *enters softly. The twilight is gone
and the moon falls through the window over*

the bed.   The hill without is bright with moonlight.]

GUIDO.   [*Softly.*]

Asleep, Lisetta?

LISETTA.

Guido!   Ah, I have need of naught, thou needst
Not leave as yet the pleasant air.

GUIDO.

Lisetta, my love, I have been long from thee.

LISETTA.

Let not that trouble thee, my needs are few,
And Pia is most kind.

GUIDO.

So little I may do.

LISETTA.

Thou hast already served to weariness.

[*He kneels beside her bed.*]

GUIDO.

My love, I have been long from thee, but now
I leave no more.   Would God these kisses might
Express the flooding of my heart!

LISETTA.

Guido, my love, perhaps I dream of thee!
Perhaps God sends a dream to solace me.

GUIDO.

Along the stream I went and where it crossed
Bevagna road—where the chestnut grows, thou
    knowest—
I saw him.

LISETTA.

Yes, yes, I know.   Whom sawest thou?

GUIDO.

The brother, Francis of Assisi.

LISETTA.

Ah, sawest thou him?

GUIDO.

Aye, him.   There had he stopped to rest; being
    spent;
And round him came the birds, beating their
    wings
Upon his robe and lighting on his arm.
Standing unseen beyond the grassy wall
I saw him smile on them and heard him speak!
"My brother birds, ye should love God who gave
To you your wings and your bright songs and
    spread
The pure wide air for you"; and stroked their
    necks
And blessed them.   And then I saw his eyes.

"Father," I cried, "speak thou to me, I faint
Beside my way!"

LISETTA.

Aye, and he said? Guido, what said he?

GUIDO.

"Thou art as one that lieth at the gate
Of Paradise and entereth not. For God
Hath given thee thy soul for its own life,
And not for glory among men."

LISETTA.

Guido!

GUIDO.

And from his deep kind eyes I drank, and knew
How God had magnified my soul through him,
And sent me peace. And I returned to thee;
For here in thee have I my glory.

LISETTA.

Now comes the old spring back again, and I
May speak! Guido, look through my window
    vines
Where the stars rise. O Love, I have not slept
For lacking thee, and oft have seen as now
The moonlight lie like sleep upon the slope,
And in the garden of the sky the moon
Drift like a blown rose. Yet I might not speak.

GUIDO.

Thou art my saint and shrine!

LISETTA.

Now shall my dream become thy song again,
And the long twilight be more sweet.

GUIDO.

I pray thee rest thee now and sleep. Goodnight.
My full heart breaks in song; and I will sit,
Hearing the blessed saints within my soul,
And will not stir from thee lest thou shouldst
    wake
When I might not be near to serve thy need.

THE DEAD POET

THE DEAD POET

THE FATHER.
THE MOTHER.
ALLEENE.
THE CHILD.

SCENE.—*A June wood, deep in a glade, with a*
slope at the back, crowned by a circle of
great trees, with thickets beyond. Yellow
primroses nestle at the foot of the slope, and
a slim path; cardinal flowers farther on,
and the call of a whippoorwill. Somewhere
the sound of a stream falling into a pool.
Twilight.

THE FATHER.

At home lies work for me, to blur my grief,
But for thy sake I walk this empty wood.

ALLEENE.

For my sake.

THE MOTHER.

Aye, here is all vain wind and idle flowers,
And there at home my hearth of joy and sorrow.
Yet for thy sake, Alleene, I linger here.

ALLEENE.

Yea, for my sake. I could not bear the house,
His house, his garden, and the hours he loved;
But here his wood also is vain and useless.

THE MOTHER.

Can we not then go home?

ALLEENE.

Aye, let us go, for here there is no promise.
The primroses like little moons do shine,
The tall trees spread cool shadows on the hill;
But he is dead.

THE MOTHER.

Mark at my breast, these three days since he
    died!
'Tis Anguish knocking there but finds it numb,
And all the chambers crowded with Pain's
    guests.

THE FATHER.

'Tis strange the child asked not to follow us.

THE MOTHER.

Where is the child, the blind child my son loved,
Pale child with drowsy hair, that loved my son?

THE FATHER.

Thou knowest we left him in the garden walk.
He is most lonely, lonelier than death.

ALLEENE.

He is most lonelier, lonelier than life.

THE FATHER.

Come, let us go, the shadows are grown long.
Our son is dead, there is no hope of solace.

ALLEENE.

Alas!

[*As they start out, the child appears among
the trees.*]

THE FATHER.

The child!

THE MOTHER.

Alas, how hast thou come?

THE CHILD.

Mine eyes alone are blind and see not.

THE MOTHER.

Art thou then lost? Where hast thou been?

THE CHILD.

I have been with him.

THE MOTHER.

Even so our grief hath likewise followed him.

THE FATHER.

Our son is dead and our hearts are dead.

THE CHILD.

Have ye not seen him?

ALLEENE.

His face is ever in my heart.

THE CHILD.

Have ye not heard him speak?

ALLEENE.

Through all my dreams his voice doth call.

THE MOTHER.

Nay, nay, what dost thou mean? And in thine
    eyes
What is there speaks? Where hast thou been,
    oh say ?

THE CHILD.

With him, with him.

THE MOTHER.

Whom dost thou mean? My son that died?

THE CHILD.

I know not whom thou meanest that died, dear
    friend;
With him that is thy son have I held speech
Amidst the forest here.

THE MOTHER.

Alas, poor youth, his fancy strays. Too hard
This wandering hath been. Come thou with us.

ALLEENE.

Thou spakest with him! Ah God! Ah God!

THE CHILD.

Grieve not!

ALLEENE.

O thou dead youth, who in thy grand desire
Took me unto thy heart, and let thy love
Fall like the rain upon my face!

THE CHILD.

Have ye not heard his voice along the grass?
The trees and pasture slope are all of him,
And the bright cardinal his passion wears!
The very seasons weave them with his moods:
Sad winter with his banners of gray moss;
And then—the stars half veiled in budding
    leaves,
The silken rhythm of the willow boughs,
Where like a glinting silk the water runs—

ALLEENE.

Aye, spring, his spring!

THE CHILD.

And then the summer—

THE MOTHER.

In summer was he born to me!

THE CHILD.

Ripe summer, when the idle folk may see
The whitening melons on their sea-green leaves.

And autumn, when beneath the hot dog-star
The earth puts off her yellow hair.

THE FATHER.

Once at that time I took my little boy
Upon my shoulder, high above the corn.

ALLEENE.

Alas, ye break me with your words! And yet,
And yet I know thou dost but dream.

THE CHILD.

Then haply thou didst love but knew him not.
Ah moods of girls, lighter than falling leaves,
The wind and vain stream carry them away!

ALLEENE.

What dost thou mean then? Speak!

THE CHILD.

He is as one with the Eternal Heart;
And in the eternal wood he takes his way,
Where no path groweth trite with human feet;
And in their holy shadow bides and marks
The cypresses of the Elysian hill.
The vagrant clouds upon their misty track
His comrades are, and in his hand he turns
The wheel of night, studded with glowing stars.

ALLEENE.

The stars he loved!

THE FATHER.

I understand thee not.

THE CHILD.

As seed restore unto the earth its own,
So he unto the elements by which he lived.

THE FATHER.

I understand thee not, and less and less;
And where my work awaits me I return.

THE MOTHER.

I will go with thee, Father.

THE CHILD.

Yea, to thy home, for there thy sorrow sits
And there thy joy hath been; and at thy hearth
Awaiteth thee, O woman, Grief, thy sister!
And thou, girl, that shalt a woman be,
Within thy room that to the meadow answers
Hide thee thy tears and in the still stars wait.

ALLEENE.

Wait!

THE CHILD.

And some day like the moon on a field of snow
The festal lamp will shine for thee again.

ALLEENE.

Never, never!

THE CHILD.

And I will come again unto him here.

For who may know when we shall meet old Pan,
Aflush with elderberries black and red;
Or in a dell the bright nymphs dancing by
Among the lucid trees!

THE FATHER.

The gods of Greece!

THE CHILD.

The high gods are not dead, the gods of Greece!
Once as we walked—ah golden memory!
Before the road's end fled the fading moon,
With one pale star, and overhead the wind
Humming like wild bees in the oak—he cried,
"The high gods are not dead! Is she not there,
Sweet silver Artemis upon the dusk?
And in the wind the wars are come again,
And great Achilles sent again to Troy!"

THE MOTHER.

How thou dost speak! The stature of thy words
Hath larger grown.

ALLEENE

Thou art his very soul!

THE FATHER.

It is the poet's fancy of my son's,
And strange to me.

THE MOTHER.

Tears blind mine eyes. Thou lovest him too.

THE FATHER.

Poor Mother!

THE MOTHER.

But still I may not follow thee.
  [*The wind blows along the grass.*]

THE CHILD.

Canst thou not hear him move amid the grass?

ALLEENE.

No, no, thou dreamest, it can not be!
  [*The wind rises in the trees overhead.*]

THE CHILD.

Mark in the tree the wind! Lo, it is twilight,
And the lone star ye have and its slim moon,
And the soft south powdered with rose!

ALLEENE.

Thou being blind alone of us dost see.

THE CHILD.

Is he not in this hour of twilight?

ALLEENE.

Nay, I hear nothing save the leaves that stir,
And the sad bird's song.

THE MOTHER.

Alas, it is all vain!

THE FATHER.

Here there is naught. We will go home, to
  mourn

And somehow to—forget.

THE MOTHER.
Nay, I can not forget—leave me my dead!

THE FATHER.
Come thou, the night is falling. Let us go.

THE CHILD.
I will return with you, and he with me,
Waiting the hour when ye shall understand:
Some hour of twinkling dawn, or wind and sun
And sway of the soft forests of the sedge,
Or yellow moon upon the azure sky,
When come the voices calling him to song.

[*They go out. The night falls in the wood.*]

THE SEVEN KINGS AND THE WIND

To

Madison Cawein

In this play an attempt is made to express divers temperaments in their search after the divine: the optimist, the idealistic philosopher, and the materialist, the East, the West, the North and the South. For the South is classic and definite, the West militant, the North mystical and tender, and the East full of dreams.

THE SEVEN KINGS AND THE WIND

THE KING OF THE EAST.
THE KING OF THE WEST.
THE KING OF THE NORTH.
THE KING OF THE SOUTH.
KING PLATON.
KING ASTAMORE.
KING FELIX.

SCENE.—*A large chamber in a palace. At the far back of the chamber a fire burns brightly, framed in a splendid fireplace of carved marbles. To the right of the fireplace is a table, spread for a feast, loaded with flagons and platters of gold and silver and crystal, with luscious fruits piled high at intervals and banked flowers. Many tapers burn, mounted in golden candelabra, on the table and on the mantelpiece. Around the table are ranged chairs, sumptuous as thrones.*

Near the front on the left is a broad bow of windows.

When the scene opens, the seven kings are

standing motionless by the window, watch-
ing. THE KING OF THE NORTH *leans his*
brow on the pane. Behind him stand THE
KING OF THE EAST *and the other kings.*
Outside the window it is black night. The fire
at the back lights dimly the front of the
chamber and the robes of the kings. Their
large shadows fall on the glass of the
windows.

THE KING OF THE NORTH.

Courage, humility and a strong heart,
O brother monarchs, is my prayer to you!
Here have we watched throughout the closing
    night,
Leaving the festal joys and the glad hearth
And jovial song and comfortable sleep,
To watch if we may see this king. Yet longer,
Longer yet, I pray! Let us not fail of hope.

KING ASTAMORE.

Is it not idle, think you, and most fond
That we should linger here in a vain search,
Parching our eyelids, chilling our warm veins,
The kings of visible delight? For me
Yonder **repast** is certain and more sweet.

KING PLATON.

Who is this king we seek?

KING ASTAMORE.

'Tis a fool's dream in his cups.

KING PLATON.

The dream must have its source. Canst thou not
say,
O King of the North, who told thee of this coming?

THE KING OF THE NORTH.

Forever by the fire I lit and fed,
And on the shadowed moors, there came to me
The rustle of a mantle more divine
Than aught I wear, though I am king; and then
Came some one calling in my chambered soul,
And now with dawn he draweth unto me.

THE KING OF THE EAST.

Beyond my dreams I heard a mystic song
Calling me unto peace beneath his wings.

THE KING OF THE SOUTH.

He will have wings then?

THE KING OF THE EAST.

Yea, pinions soft as sleep, beneath their folds
Eternal twilight and oblivion.

KING PLATON.

The realms beyond this palace we know not.
Haply he bringeth tidings of new thought;

I needs must wait with patience lest by chance
This be no dream, and he should come.

THE KING OF THE WEST.
Perhaps he is a king of power and glory
Whose realms surpass our utmost speculation.

KING PLATON.
How if he yet is climbing to himself,
Aeons and aeons of struggle to the Whole.

KING ASTAMORE.
Then he is not yet born, think you?

KING PLATON.
Born but not yet perfect.

THE KING OF THE SOUTH.
I would see beauty and perfection crowned.

KING FELIX.
I know not how it be, but through the night
My heart hath not grown heavy. I feast, I wait,
Doubting no whit that he will come; therefore
I have found solace and some joy and hope.

KING PLATON.
Thy happiness hath thought for thee, thy flesh
Hath cheered thee on.

THE KING OF THE SOUTH.
Ah nay, the saddened eye looks down, O King!

Clear vision comes of joy and a high heart.

THE KING OF THE NORTH.

Did I not know, did I not know!—the light
Brightens and brightens and the wind hath risen.
Come, O brothers, to me here and know!

[*The kings draw near the window and watch
together in silence. Slowly the dawn grows
through the window and a faint light enters
the room. The fire at the back flickers and
slowly dies.*]

THE KING OF THE NORTH.

I see a kingdom mantled with bright mist,
And forms I have no words to name.

KING PLATON.

That which I cannot name I see not.

THE KING OF THE NORTH.

Do ye not hear?

KING PLATON.

What dost thou hear?

THE KING OF THE EAST.

The music of his coming.

KING PLATON.

I hear the wind blowing on the ramparts there.

THE KING OF THE NORTH.

Dimly I see the hills of my desire.

KING PLATON.

'Tis thine idea's incorporeal mate,
The Being of thy Becoming.

THE KING OF THE EAST.

Hollow and vain is thy philosophy
At such an hour, most hollow and most vain.

THE KING OF THE NORTH.

I see a spirit there, a form and face
Mistier than dawn and lovelier than dawn
And hosts of shadowy angels clouding him!

KING PLATON.

Methought that once I saw as thou.   'Tis gone
And reason speaks.   It cannot be.

THE KING OF THE EAST.

His shape is in mine eyes but I am blind,
His name is in my mouth but I am dumb.

KING ASTAMORE.   [*Coming forward.*]

Brothers, behold I slept and in my sleep
I dreamed, and on the wind I saw a presence
Hedged with fire.

THE KING OF THE EAST.

Hearken!   Speak thou, O king!

KING PLATON.

'Twas in thy dream.

KING ASTAMORE.

And now I waken and do know my folly,
For there is naught.

THE KING OF THE EAST.

Discredit not thy dream too soon.

THE KING OF THE NORTH.

Alas, seest thou no light?

KING ASTAMORE.

I see the candles of the banquet there.

KING FELIX.

Ah, woe, our candles die down!

KING ASTAMORE.

There is no other light.

KING PLATON.

There is no other light than we ourselves
Have made, no other.

THE KING OF THE EAST.

O blinder than the charring embers, look!
Can ye not see the splendor riding there?
There in a cloud set round with burning plumes,
A heart of fire; and to him little flames
Rise up and enter his great radiance,
Like men from other realms.

THE KING OF THE WEST.

What other realms, dear brother?

KING ASTAMORE.
There be no realms but this.

KING PLATON.
Are there men within that darkness?

THE KING OF THE EAST.
I see their souls.

THE KING OF THE NORTH.
Look thou, I see his form, dark, robed like us.

KING PLATON.
'Tis thy own shadow there thou seest.

KING FELIX.
Look how our shadows fade to less and less!
[*The lights die down.*]

THE KING OF THE SOUTH.
Fairer he moves than fire or any cloud;
All that mine eye hath dreamed of loveliness,
The mold of strength and the ideal grace,
The spacious forehead and ambrosial brow!
Behold his advent and the hosts about
In order and perfection ranged.

THE KING OF THE NORTH.
Hearest thou the wind speak?

THE KING OF THE SOUTH.
I do hear naught but glory.

KING ASTAMORE.

Madmen, madmen all!

THE KING OF THE WEST.

Perchance, O king, the glass set there before us
Hinders our guest.

THE KING OF THE EAST.

Nay, nay, break not the glass while burn the
candles!

THE KING OF THE WEST.

Haply we learned to scorn our candlelight.
If he should come in glory.

KING FELIX.

Break not the glass. Woe, woe, woe, forever,
The eternal chill is there!

THE KING OF THE NORTH.

The perfect and ideal light is there.

KING PLATON.

Reach forth thy hand and break then.

THE KING OF THE NORTH.

Nay, still I dare not.

KING PLATON.

Then will I dare, for I will know.
[*He shatters the glass. The wind rushes in
and the candles go out. The kings fall on*

*their knees, and huddle together in a corner
of the window.*]

KING ASTAMORE.
Alas, I see not either candlelight or dawn!

KING PLATON.
Alas, I die and have not seen the king!

A VOICE IN THE WIND.
He is so much as thou dost apprehend,
The rest for thee is but the Universe.

THE QUEEN OF SHEBA

To

Clayton Hamilton

*"In grateful remembrance of their youth and
their already old affection."*

THE QUEEN OF SHEBA

AUVERGNE, *who thinks himself to be King Solo-mon.*

GAWAIN, *who thinks himself the Prince of Wales.*

ADELLE, *who, for a time, thinks herself the Queen of Sheba.*

A SISTER, *their keeper.*

SCENE.—*A Gothic chamber, spacious and shadowy, the long windows at the far end heavily curtained. Through the curtains the downs appear, broken by rocky crags. Far below is a mere, and the sound of the water in the coves mingles with the wind from the moor. The curtains move faintly with the shifting wind.*

It is the King's harem. The walls are fantas-tically covered with pictures of women in many styles. On the table and over the floor lie a number of pictures cut in two.

AUVERGNE *stands on the right, dressed as King Solomon in state, with a long sweeping mantle and a crown of faded gilt. To the*

121

left of the door in the rear, stands GAWAIN,
in a servile attitude almost curlike.

AUVERGNE.

That thou, Wales, mayst enter here, we grant;
But thou mayst not draw near unto our person.
For ranged with ours, thy lineage is humble;
William the Norman, thy first ancestor,
Though lord of Britain, was meanwhile the son
Of a low peasant woman—therefore thou,
Not through thy fathers' nor thine own desert,
Mayst look upon our face in presence here,
But through our courtesy.

GAWAIN.

La, la, I know well the dead leaves fall.

AUVERGNE.

Poor brutish knave! Go thou and bear this
    word:
The Queen of Sheba is most welcome.

[GAWAIN *shambles out. The door is reopened
    and* ADELLE *enters. She wears a torn veil
    and glitters with ornaments. In her hand
    she carries an old wreath of wax flowers and
    with it a cluster of faded roses.* GAWAIN
    *follows her and takes his former place by
    the door at the back. The* SISTER *attendant
    enters and stations herself near the door.*]

AUVERGNE.

Who is she that looketh forth as the morning?

ADELLE.

I am a rose of Sharon,
A lily of the valleys.

AUVERGNE.

As a lily among thorns
So art thou among the daughters.

ADELLE.

As the apple tree among the trees of the wood,
So art thou among the sons.

AUVERGNE.

There are threescore queens
And fourscore concubines
And virgins without number,
But thou art one.

SISTER.

Ah, blessed God, how beautiful are they!
Alas, this heavy madness!

ADELLE.

From mine own far-off realm I come, O King,
For marvel of thy name.

AUVERGNE.

Soft is thy voice as when the twilight falls
On Lebanon, and the dove calls.

ADELLE.

Weary my feet and weary my starved eyes
For sight of thee, Beloved.

SISTER.

How the wind wails on the moorland!

AUVERGNE.

Sweeter than honey from the cedar wood
Thy coming is, fairer than stars thy sight:
Yet unto me some twice or thrice hast thou
Seemed strange—though I have half forgot.

ADELLE.

Alas, I know not how it was.   Meseemed
That sudden I was not, another stood
Here in my place, and looked on thee and feared;
Finding thee strange and far, and all thy glory
Mocked and made hideous.   Then there came fire
And flame across my brain.

AUVERGNE.

And then?

ADELLE.

Then once again I saw thee as thou art,
Even as thou standest here in majesty.

AUVERGNE.

That time I lost thee was the world to me
A darkness and a night.

ADELLE.

Darkness and fire was it to me!

AUVERGNE.

Sit thou and rest, 'tis past. [*She seats herself
near him.*]

ADELLE.

Certain I am not well. Behind mine eyes
Fire and ice succeed each other. Nay,
'Tis gone.

AUVERGNE.

'Tis not the old disease, think you?

ADELLE.

Let me not think on it. Behold, my lord,
Here have I brought thee flowers from the vale,
Little blue lilies from the water brooks,
And roses drowned with dew; and mingled here
Are petals all of wax, which I have done,
Weaving therein the summer of my love.

AUVERGNE.

Star of the South, we render thanks to thee.

ADELLE.

Perfect are they, most perfect each to each,
As are our loves. Then wilt thou not, O King,
Make trial of thy wisdom? Which is wax,
And which the rain and sun?

[AUVERGNE *goes to the window and opens it.*]

AUVERGNE.

Come hither, tiny arbiters of the air,
Winged seekers of God's sweetness through the
    world,
And solve my riddle.

ADELLE.

Look, the clouds break! The sun, O King!

AUVERGNE.

The sun? [ADELLE *stands by the window and
    looks at the sun. The bees come in at the
    window.*]
Behold, they settle where the rose is sweet.
Did I not know, sweetness and truth are one?
Look how the bees have judged. Alas,
That in this world men know not true from false,
I know it not, tho I am king.

    [*Suddenly* ADELLE *tears away her veil and
    shrieks.*]

ADELLE.

Oh, oh!

AUVERGNE.

What ails my queen? Hath the sun maddened
    thee?

ADELLE.

That fire again! And now a stranger walks

Within the chamber of my brain, to drive
Me hence. A woman like to me but strange.
Oh!—come thou not near me—touch me not!
Help, Sister! [*She runs toward the door at the
back.*]

SISTER.

Daughter——

ADELLE.

Save me, O God, save me!

SISTER.

Nay, calm thee, calm thee, what seest thou?

ADELLE.

I saw a cloud pass from the earth! Look, look,
Oh, am I mad,—or is it he that's mad?
Is it not he, my cousin, there, Auvergne?
That walks distractedly with robe and crown
In mockery of state? Is 't not Gawain,
The poor fool sobbing by the door, whose face
Is like a beast's? [GAWAIN *wails as he crouches
by the door.*]

AUVERGNE.

Silence thy crying in our court, thou dog!
Who is this woman glowering at me
That rends our court with noise?

SISTER.

Wilt thou not come with me?

ADELLE.

Look where his great eyes burn like stars! Alas,
Sister, I fear him.

SISTER.

Fear not.

ADELLE.

That veil, these rings—O, Christ, I see at last!
I was as that, and Thou hast shriven me,
O horrible, most horrible!

AUVERGNE.

Depart, out of my sight, give place, give place,
Lest I should drive ye forth——

SISTER.

Come——

ADELLE.

Auvergne, alas, Auvergne!
   [ADELLE *and the* SISTER *hasten out, and*
   GAWAIN *follows them, cowering with fear.*
   AUVERGNE *falls on his knees by the window,*
   beating his breast.]

AUVERGNE.

Hear, me, O God, alone I turn to Thee,
Let not the honor of Thy servant fail,
Let not my glory nor my kingdom pass.

What is that face upon the wind, O God?
Whither is my Beloved fled, oh, whither!

ACT II.

Seven days have passed. The windows are
dark. Outside, the wind around the towers
eddies and moans, and brings the sound of
breakers and far-off danger bells. The
flame of the candles in the chamber burns
steady and straight.

AUVERGNE *lies propped on his pillow, his eyes*
closed. At the back of the room, GAWAIN
crouches against the wall, muttering to him-
self. ADELLE *and the* SISTER *attendant stand*
watching at the bedside.

ADELLE.

Alas, he hath lain so these seven days,
Shattered and moaning, and his weary heart
Stolen from him into the vales of Sheba!

SISTER.

How perfect is this shadow unto him.

ADELLE.

Surely, O Sister, these imaginings,
These images of life, and life are one.

SISTER.

God doeth all things well.

ADELLE.

I know not easily this God of yours.
The cloud He sent on me hath rendered Him
Shadowy, blurred, an image like the rest.

SISTER.

Hush, child, thou speakest rashly.

ADELLE.

Is 't justly done, think you, that on this man
Fall Doom and Death where other men escape.

SISTER.

Hath he not had his joys also? For God
Evens the scales of life.

ADELLE.

Have I not told thee how, while yet a boy,
He could not rein his soaring heart, but sped
Like a white star, feeding upon itself.
His mind was as a heaven of golden fires,
And there beyond lurked darkness and the void.
Wisdom he chose, the cloudy heights of thought,
And following there, so snapped the chord that
     bound
His feet to the common earth, and reason
     failed—
Reason the traitor failed him in his need.

SISTER.

Reason is soonest spared. Sooner than love,

Hope, and the unfailing trust.

ADELLE.

Wherefore pursuing wisdom he becomes
Wise Solomon, and is no more Auvergne,
My mother's cousin. And his kingly thought,
Above the dun realities of fact,
Hath seen the glory of the world and drunk
The wine of dreams—how mid his sorry state,
Hath majesty, enthroned within his thought,
Made glorious the record of his days!

SISTER.

The glory and the pomp of shadows.

ADELLE.

The ideal grace, the unsullied Orient
Are his.

SISTER.

Have I not seen this splendor?

ADELLE.

Yea, faithful thou hast been through all the
     years
To him and him and—and to me, when I
Grovelled and bit the dust of shame.

GAWAIN. [*At the back.*]

Our cousin grants us leave to make our shroud,
Shall not the glowworm light my chamber then?

[*Sings.*]
His shadow moveth to his grave,
    Kneel where he lies, ladie,
His cold lips kiss the ear of death,
    Close down his eyes, ladie!

SISTER.

Poor, poor wretch!

ADELLE.

God's justice toucheth not his case, this child,
This thriving death, my cousin Gawain there.
He hath not lived, but entered life as dead.

GAWAIN.

Let them not fall, lo, there are leaves, black
    leaves,
Falling, down through the air upon his bed.

SISTER.   [*Touching his arm.*]
Hush, thy cousin lies dying!

GAWAIN.

Canst thou not light more candles?

SISTER.

'Tis light here.   There darkness lies, beyond.

GAWAIN.

Sister, beyond the window, look, oh, look,
I see the souls of men shuddering in darkness.

AUVERGNE.

Who is she that looketh forth as the morning?
The rose of Sharon, the lily of the valleys?
My Beloved is gone from me and hath departed.
As a lily among thorns, so was my love
Among the daughters, oh, return, return,
That I may look upon thee.

ADELLE.

Alas, canst thou not sleep?

AUVERGNE.

The glory of my court is gone.

ADELLE.

Auvergne, Auvergne, Auvergne, thou hast but
    dreamed—
Cousin, thou hast but dreamed.

AUVERGNE.

There are threescore queens and virgins without
    number,
But she is one.   Seest thou not there
The women dead for my Beloved's sake?

ADELLE.

I see but pictures cut in twain, Auvergne.
Thou wanderest in a dream.

AUVERGNE.

My Beloved is mine till the day break

And the shadows flee away.
Oh, return, return that I may look upon thee.

ADELLE.

Can naught be done?

SISTER.

Nothing.

AUVERGNE.

Send me mine end, O God, weary am I,
Weary and most weary of my realm.

ADELLE.

Naught?

SISTER.

Naught.

AUVERGNE.

Wilt thou not come again?

ADELLE.

Spare me, O God, spare me, O God! Do Thou
Let me be mad again to comfort him,
For I have killed him.

SISTER.

Nay, thou hast not killed him!

AUVERGNE.

Day after day, and weary years are come,
But not my love.

ADELLE.

Show me O God, how I may come to him!

SISTER.

Perhaps the garments thou didst wear, the veil—
If thou wouldst put them on again——

ADELLE.

The garments of my shame, oh, never, never,—
To wrap my flesh in madness once again
And shame——

SISTER.

Pray thee heed not my foolish words, my
    daughter,
Strayed was my thought—to comfort him—I did
Forget thine agony.

AUVERGNE.

What is my sin, O Lord, that thou hast sent
This sorrow on me?

ADELLE.

Madness again, I cannot, oh, I cannot——

AUVERGNE.

Alas, forever and forever——

ADELLE.

I must, I will, though I be wrapped with flame!
Speak thou to him.

SISTER.

I may not speak for tears.

ADELLE.

O King, O Solomon, hear me, even now
She cometh out of Sheba.

AUVERGNE.

Open the gates that she may enter in,
Open the gates to my Beloved.

[ADELLE *goes out.*]

AUVERGNE.

Look forth, Beloved, on Jerusalem,
Lo, where the towers and the gilded spires
Make lightnings of the moon, and the night lies
Softer than sleep upon the town.   A star
Is in the west, sinking; but thou art mine.
As the moon amid the fading stars art thou
Among the daughters, O Beloved!

GAWAIN.

Is the king sick unto death?

SISTER.

His eyes are glassed with death already.
    [ADELLE *enters with the veil and wreath. She*
    falls on her knees beside him, and beats her
    breast.]

ADELLE.   .

Here, here am I, here, here beside thee—Sheba!

SISTER.

His eyes move not.

ADELLE.

What have I done? Let me be mad in truth,
Madness again were better than this pain.

GAWAIN.   [*Breaking into a laugh.*]
Ha, ha, I see a flame upon the mere
That bloweth seaward.

SISTER.

Hush, Gawain!

GAWAIN.

The little soul flickers on the wave.

ADELLE.

Lo, I am come, O King, the Queen of Sheba!

SISTER.

He hears thee not.   Hearken the wind!

AUVERGNE.

Mark how the trumpets blow around the walls,
I will go out to meet my love.

ADELLE.

Alas, that I were mad, for I have slain him!
Auvergne, Prince!   King!—O God—!

SISTER.

He hears thee not, his eyes are set.

AUVERGNE.

Till the day break and the shadows flee away,
Oh, return, return, that I may look upon thee.

DATE DUE
